Set at the foot of the magnificent rolling Mendip Hills in Somerset, Wells is the smallest city in England, and one of the most beautiful in Britain. Its name is derived from springs which rise close to the Bishop's Palace: fed from the Mendip Caves system, they never run dry.

Wells is full of history with much to see, and it would be difficult to do justice to it with just one day's visit. Visitors are well catered for with a variety of hotels and ancient inns.

Wells developed as a religious site over the centuries, and the tiny city has grown around its Cathedral, in contrast to the more usual sequence where a place of worship is built to serve an already established settlement.

Apart from the City of Wells, there are a host of other interesting places to visit within a short distance. We hope that this guide book will enhance your stay and serve as a reminder of a very pleasant visit.

Dans le magnifique paysage vallonné des Mendips Hills du Somerset, Wells, bien que la plus petite, est l'une des plus belles villes de Grande-Bretagne. Cette ville qui tire son nom des trois sources situées à proximité du palais épiscopal, est très étroitement associée à la ville toute proche de Bath aux sources thermales chaudes. Ensemble, elles constituent le diocèse de Bath et Wells.

Wells regorge de monuments historiques bien entretenus, et il est difficile de tout voir en une seule journée.

A part la ville de Wells, il y a toute une multitude d'endroits intéressants à visiter à courte distance. Nous espérons que ce guide vous permettra de mieux apprécier votre séjour et sera le souvenir d'une visite très agréable.

Wells, das inmitten der herrlichen, sanften Mendip-Hügel Somersets liegt, ist zwar die kleinste, aber auch eine der schönsten Städte Großbritanniens. Ihr Name stammt von drei Quellen in der Nähe des bischöflichen Palais und ist mit der nahegelegenen Stadt Bath, die heiße Quellen hat, eng verbunden. Diese beiden Städte sind tatsächlich in de Diözese von Bath und Wells verbunden.

Wells ist voll von gut erhaltenen historischen Sehenswürdigkeiten, und es ist schwer, ihr mit einem Tagesbesuch gerecht zu werden.

Abgesehen von der Stadt Wells gibt es in der nahegelegenen Umgebung viele andere interessante Orte zu besichtigen. Wir hoffen, dass dieser Führer Ihren Aufenthalt bereichern und Ihnen als Erinnerung an einen wunderschönen Besuch dienen wird.

THE CATHEDRAL

Wells Cathedral has been described as a jewel in the crown of English cathedrals. Its great West Front of c.1240 (photograph right) with nearly 300 surviving carved figures, is the largest collection of figure sculpture of its date in the western world. Wells Cathedral was built on what had been a religious site beside the springs or 'wells' since at least the earliest days of Christianity in Britain. A late Roman burial-place and Saxon chapels were found during excavations in 1978.

In about 705 AD a church was founded here by Aldhelm, Bishop of Sherborne. In 909 it was granted cathedral status. The construction of the present Cathedral church was started in about 1180 and dedicated in 1239. Important additions were made in the 14th and 15th centuries. The South Cloister, completed in 1508, was the last part to be added although of course additions and alterations have been made over the years, and conservation work continues today.

The Cathedral is built of cream coloured Inferior Oolite stone, which comes from a quarry at Doulting, about 8 miles away. 'Inferior' means that it comes from a layer below the Greater Oolite, which is the finer, whiter Bath stone. Doulting stone has been used in recent years to build Guildford Cathedral.

Ever since Richard I was crowned King of England at Westminster Abbey in 1189, the Bishop of Bath and Wells has had the special privilege of supporting the monarch on his or her left side at the coronation, while the Bishop of Durham stands on the right side.

LA CATHÉDRALE DE WELLS a été décrite comme le fleuron de la couronne parmi les cathédrales anglaises. Sa grande façade O. (vers 1240) (photo ci-dessus) est décorée de près de 300 statues subsistantes. C'est la plus importante collection de sculptures de figurines datant de cette époque dans le monde occidental. La cathédrale de Wells fut construite sur un emplacement religieux, situé à côté d'une source ou "puits" (wells, en anglais), depuis les premiers jours de la chrétienté en Grande-Bretagne.

La construction de l'actuelle cathédrale commença vers l'an 1180, mais elle fut consacrée en 1239. D'importantes ajouts vinrent la compléter aux 14e et 15e siècles, notamment le cloître sud, achevé en 1508, qui fut la dernière partie à venir s'ajouter, mais d'autres annexes et altérations y furent apportées au fil des ans. Les travaux de conservation se poursuivent encore aujourd'hui.

DIE KATHEDRALE von Wells wurde als Juwel in der Krone der englischen Kathedralen beschrieben. Ihre großartige westliche Vorderseite, die ca.1240 erbaut wurde (Foto oben) weist nahezu 300 erhalten gebliebene geschnitze Figuren auf und ist die größte Sammlung von Figurskulpturen ihrer Zeit in der westlichen Welt. Die Kathedrale von Wells wurde neben den Quellen oder "Brunnen" (Wells) auf einem Grund erbaut, der schon seit den frühesten Anfängen des christlichen Glaubens in Großbritannien religiösen Zwecken diente.

Die Konstruktion der gegenwärtigen Kirchenkathedrale begann ungefähr im Jahre 1180 und wurde 1239 eingeweiht. Wichtige Anbauten wurden im 14ten und 15ten Jahrhundert vollzogen. Der südliche Kreuzgang, der 1508 fertiggestellt wurde, war der letzte Anbau, wenn auch Erweiterungen und Veränderungen immer wieder vorgenommen wurden und Instandhaltungsarbeiten auch heute noch stattfinden.

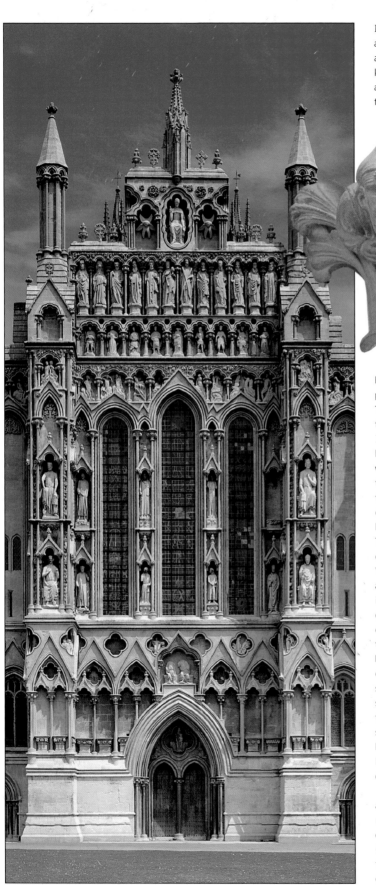

In 1088 the bishop's throne (the cathedra from which a cathedral takes its name) was moved to Bath Abbey and Wells ceased to be a cathedral. The Bishop was known as the Bishop of Bath. In 1219 Bishop Jocelyn applied to the Pope to have cathedral status restored to Wells. The building of the present cathedral at Wells was undertaken as part of this campaign. The Pope made extensive enquiries about Wells' origins as a cathedral, and the Saxon bishops of Wells. Negotiations took a long time, and it was only in 1245 that Bishop Roger, Jocelyn's successor, finally became Bishop of Bath and Wells. The two great churches were joint cathedrals until Bath Abbey was dissolved in 1539.

On entering the Nave of Wells Cathedral (photograph right), visitors are immediately impressed by the uninterrupted rhythm of the sturdy early Gothic pillars and arches, the triforium and the high vault. The scissor arches (photograph page 6) under the tower are an outstanding feature.

In 1338, after the central tower had been heightened, there was a near disaster when the tower began to crack as the foundations could not cope with the extra height and weight. The Master Mason or architect, William Joy, devised a brilliant solution in the scissor arches on three sides of the crossing under the tower. Constructed between 1338 and c.1348, they have successfully stabilised the central tower and, supplemented by hidden buttresses, kept it safe to this day.

In both Nave and Transepts are pillars with carved capitals; realistic and fantastic birds and animals, biblical and everyday figures, including 'the Toothache Man' (photograph above). In the South Transept is the famous carving of the grape stealers, in four episodes all round one pillar.

En entrant dans la nef de la cathédrale de Wells (photo page 5), les visiteurs sont immédiatement frappés par l'harmonie ininterrompue des piliers et des arches robustes, le triforium et la haute voûte de style gothique primitif. Les arcs de décharge inversés (photo à gauche) sous la tour constituent un motif exceptionnel. En 1338, après le rehaussement de la tour, une catastrophe fut à craindre: la tour commença à se fendre car les fondations ne pouvaient pas supporter la hauteur et le poids additionnels. Le maître d'oeuvre ou architecte, William Joy, trouva une solution géniale en construisant des arcs de décharge inversés sur les trois côtés de la croisée du transept, sous la tour. Construites entre 1338 et environ 1348, elles ont réussi à stabiliser la tour centrale et avec en plus des arc-boutants dissimulés, elles ont réussi à la préserver jusqu'à ce jour.

Dans la nef et les transepts, les piliers sont surmontés de chapiteaux sculptés d'oiseaux et d'animaux naturels ou imaginaires, des personnages de la bible ou de la vie courante, notamment "l'homme au mal de dents" (photo page 4). Dans le transept sud, se trouve la célèbre sculpture des voleurs de raisins en quatre épisodes tout autour du pilier.

Beim Betreten des Hauptschiffes der Kathedrale von Wells (Foto Seite 5) sind Besucher unmittelbar vom fortlaufenden Rhythmus der stabilen Säulen und der Bögen der frühen Gothik, dem Triforium und den hohen Gewölben, beeindruckt. Die Scherenbögen (Foto links) unter dem Turm sind ein hervorragendes Merkmal. Nachdem der zentrale Turm im Jahre 1338, erhöht wurde, gab es beinahe eine Katastrophe, als der Turm Risse bekam, weil das Fundament für die zusätzliche Höhe und das Gewicht nicht stabil genug war. Der Steinmetzmeister und Architekt William Joy erbrachte eine ausgezeichnete Lösung mit den Scherenbögen auf drei Seiten der Kreuzung unter dem Turm. Sie wurden von 1338 bis 1348 gebaut und haben den zentralen Turm erfolgreich stabilisiert und, unterstützt durch verdeckte Strebepfeiler bis heute stabil erhalten.

Sowohl im Haupt- als auch im Querschiff befinden sich Säulen mit geschnitzten Kapitellen; realistische und Phantasievögel und -tiere, biblische und alltägliche Figuren, einschließlich des "Zahnschmerz-Mannes" (Foto Seite 4). Im südlichen Querschiff befindet sich die berühmte Schnitzerei der Traubendiebe die sich in vier Episoden um die gesamte Säule windet.

Perhaps the best known of the Cathedral's many treasures is the clock (photographs right) which was installed c.1390 and was first mentioned in records in 1392. It has the oldest original clock-dial still in existence. The works of the Salisbury Cathedral clock are a few years older, c.1386, and were made by the same clockmaker as those of Wells, which are now on view, still working, in the Science Museum in London. The present works of the Wells clock were installed in 1880.

As the inside clock strikes every quarter of an hour, the quarter-jack, Jack Blandiver (photograph below), kicks his heels to ring the bells. On the hour he strikes the bell in front of him. Above the clock dials, four knights on horseback chase each other round, and one knight is knocked over at each revolution.

Wells Cathedral has some very fine glass of the 1300s in the tracery (or upper) lights of the Quire Aisles, and particularly in the Quire itself. The great Jesse window (c.1340) at the east end of the Quire is often called the Golden Window from its glowing colours (photograph page 4). In the Lady chapel a jigsaw of medieval glass fragments fills most of the windows, showing how much magnificent colour has been lost from the rest of the Cathedral - perhaps broken deliberately at the Reformation, or by Oliver Cromwell's soldiers, or lost through neglect.

Le plus connu des nombreux trésors de la cathédrale est peut-être son horloge (photo ci-dessus) qui fut installée vers 1390 et mentionnée pour la première fois dans les archives, en 1392. C'est la plus ancienne horloge originale à cadran en existence. Le mécanisme actuel de la pendule de Wells fut installé en 1880.

L'horloge intérieure sonne tous les quarts d'heure. Le jaquemart, Jack Blandiver (photo à gauche) donne un coup de pied sur les cloches. A l'heure, il frappe la cloche devant lui. Au-dessus des cadrans de l'horloge, quatre chevaliers à cheval se poursuivent en cercle, un chevalier étant renversé à chaque tour.

La cathédrale de Wells possède de magnifiques vitraux datant du 13e siècle dans les entrelacs (tympan) de la rosace des allées du choeur, et particulièrement dans le choeur proprement dit. Le grand vitrail de Jessé (vers 1340) à l'extrémité E. du choeur est souvent désigné par le nom de Vitrail d'or à cause de ses couleurs resplendissantes (photo page 4). Dans la chapelle de la Vierge, un puzzle de fragments de vitraux du moyen-âge remplit la plupart des baies, donnant un aperçu des coloris magnifiques qui ont disparu du reste de la cathédrale.

vollen Stunden schlägt er die Glocke, die sich direkt vor ihm befindet. über dem Zifferblatt jagen sich vier Ritter auf Pferden gegenseitig im Kreis herum, und bei jeder vollen Runde wird ein Ritter umgestoßen.

Die Wells Kathedrale besitzt sehr wertvolles Glas aus dem 13ten Jahrhundert im Maßwerk (den oberen Fenstern) der Chorgänge und besonders im Chor selbst. Das große Jesse-Fenster, (ca.1340) auf der Ostseite des Chors wird oft wegen seiner leuchtenden Farben das "Goldene Fenster" genannt (Foto Seite 4). In der Marienkapelle füllt ein Mosaik aus mittelalterlichen Glasstücken die meisten Fenster aus und zeigt dadurch die großartige Farbenpracht, die in den anderen Teilen der Kathedrale verloren gegangen ist.

Der Chor (Foto links) ist mit dem Thron des Bishofs, dem mit farbenprächtigen Stickereien geschmückten Gestühl der Kanoniker und dem hölzernen Chorgestühl davor das Herz der Kathedrale. Unter den Sitzen dieses Chorgestühls befinden sich verschlungene, fein geschnitzte hölzerne Zierleisten, die Misericords genannt werden. Diese wurden zum größten Teil um 1333 fertiggestellt. Wenn die Sitze während der langen mittelalterlichen Gottesdienste hochgeklappt wurden, konnten die Chormitglieder sich diskret auf diesen Leisten ausruhen, während es so aussah, als ob sie aufrecht stehen würden. Der Name kommt von dem lateinischen Wort misericordia: "habe Mitleid" - habe Mitleid mit den schmerzenden Beinen der Chormitglieder. Da die Misericords normalerweise nicht zu sehen sind, sind drei davon in der Südost-Ecke an der äußeren Wand des Chors ausgestellt, so dass die exquisiten Einzelheiten der Schnitzerei bei guter Beleuchtung zu erkennen sind.

Die Turmuhr (Foto Seite 7) ist wahrscheinlich einer der berühmtesten Kunstschätze der Kathedrale. Sie wurde etwa 1390 installiert und 1392 zum ersten Mal in schriftlichen Aufzeichnungen erwähnt. Sie hat das älteste Zifferblatt, das heute noch im Originalzustand existiert. Das gegenwärtige Uhrwerk der Wellsuhr wurde 1880 eingesetzt.

Jack Blandiver (Foto Seite 7), der Glockenschläger, schlägt alle viertel Stunde seine Hacken zusammen, um die Glocken zu läuten. Bei

The Quire (photograph left) is the heart of the Cathedral, with the bishop's throne, the canons' stalls hung with colourful embroideries, and the wooden choirstalls in front. Underneath the seats of these choirstalls are intricately carved wooden ledges called misericords, mostly made c.1333. When the seats were tipped up during the long medieval services, the occupants could discreetly rest themselves on these ledges while still appearing to stand upright. The names comes from the Latin misericordia: "have pity" - have pity on a canon's aching legs. As the misericords cannot normally be seen, three of them are displayed on the outer wall of the quire at its south-east corner, in a good light where the exquisite detail of the carving can be clearly seen.

A magnificent staircase (photograph above) curves up to the first floor Chapter House. The staircase was begun about 1240, and the Chapter House finally completed in 1306. The stairway windows contain the oldest stained glass in the Cathedral, c.1290. The Chapter house was the "place of business" for the Chapter, the collective name for the Dean and Canons who are responsible for running the Cathedral. This beautiful octagonal room has huge windows containing some originals roundels of stained glass which show Resurrection scenes. The roof is a feat of medieval engineering, a 32-rib vault supported on a single central pillar. Around the walls are the canons' stalls or seats, each with its own nameplate. The full Chapter now only meets here on special occasions.

The Cathedral Library over the East Cloister was built c.1425, and is one of the longest of its date in England. The present bookshelves, desks and panelling were fit

Le choeur (photo page 8) se trouve au centre de la cathédrale, avec le trône de l'évêque, les bancs des chanoines ornés de broderies chatoyantes, et les bancs de bois du choeur à l'avant. Sous les sièges de ces stalles, des bords en bois aux sculptures délicates, désignés sous le nom de miséricordes, datent presque tous de 1333 env. Lorsque les sièges étaient renversés pendant les longues messes médiévales, les occupants pouvaient discrètement se reposer sur ces bords tout en faisant semblant de se tenir debout. Le nom vient du latin misericordia "ayez pitié" - pitié des pauvres jambes des chanoines. Comme normalement, les miséricordes ne sont pas exposées, on a cloué trois d'entre elles sur le mur extérieur du choeur dans le coin S.-E. en pleine lumière pour mieux pouvoir admirer le travail délicat de la sculpture.

Un escalier magnifique (photo page 9) se déroule jusqu'au premier étage de la salle capitulaire. Cet escalier fut commencé vers 1240, et la salle capitulaire fut achevée en 1306. Les fenêtres de l'escalier contiennent les plus anciens vitraux de la cathédrale (vers 1290). C'était dans la salle capitulaire que se déroulaient les "affaires" du chapitre, ce nom recouvrant le doyen et les chanoines responsables de la gestion de la cathédrale. Le toit est un exemple magnifique de l'ingéniosité des bâtisseurs du moyen-âge, avec sa voûte aux 32 nervures reposant sur un unique pilier central. Les sièges ou stalles des chanoines tapissent les murs, chacun portant le nom de son occupant.

La bibliothèque de la cathédrale située au-dessus du coté E. du cloître fut construite vers 1425. C'est l'une des plus longues de cette époque en Angleterre. Les étagères, bureaux et lambris actuels furent installés en 1685-86.

Ein eindrucksvoller Treppenaufgang (Foto Seite 9) windet sich zum im ersten Stockwerk gelegenen Kapitelsaal hinauf. Der Bau des Treppenaufgangs wurde etwa 1240 begonnen. 1306 wurde schließlich der Kapitelsaal fertig gestellt. Die Fenster im Treppenaufgang enthalten das älteste farbige Glas der Kathedrale (ca. 1290). Der Kapitelsaal war das "Zentrum des Geschehens" für das Kapitel, ein Sammelbegriff für den Dekan und die Kanoniker, die für die Verwaltung der Kathedrale die Verantwortung tragen. Das Dach ist eine Leistung mittelalterlicher Ingenieurskunst, ein Gewölbe mit 32 Rippen, die auf einer einzigen zentralen Säule ruhen. An den Wänden sind die Sitze der Kanoniker, die alle mit persönlichen Namensschildern versehen sind.

Die Bücherei der Kathedrale über dem östlichen Kreuzgang wurde ca. 1425 erbaut und ist eine der räumlich längsten ihrer Zeit in England. Die heute vorhandenen Bücherregale, Schreibtische und Vertäfelungen wurden 1685/86 eingebaut.

BISHOP'S PALACE

Bishop Jocelyn (1206-1242), who was born in Wells, built the present central hall of the Palace and also established a deer park close by.

Later Bishops made various additions, particularly Bishop Burnell (1275-1292) who added the Great Hall and Chapel.

Following a dispute with the townspeople of Wells, Bishop Ralph of Shrewsbury (1329-1363) built the surrounding walls, with gatehouse, drawbridge and moat (photograph below). The moat contains an interesting variety of water birds, including the famous swans who have learned to ring a bell when they want food (photograph below).

The Palace (photograph top right page 12) is open to visitors from spring to autumn, and holds "open days" for various fund-raising charity events. It is also available to hire for wedding receptions, corporate dinners, conferences, seminars and outside events such as concerts and theatre productions.

The Palace gardens extend to an area of about fourteen acres and consist of a magnificent collection of lawns, flowers, shrubs and trees (photograph pages 13-14). On the central lawn, where there is a black walnut tree nearly two hundred years old, the Palace Croquet Club plays during the summer months (photograph page 13).

LE PALAIS ÉPISCOPAL: C'est à l'évêque Jocelin qui naquit à Wells, que l'on attribue l'amorce de la construction du palais au 13e siècle où il créa un parc pour abriter un "camera" ou appartements d'habitation.

D'autres bâtiments annexes furent érigés par une succession d'évêques, surtout l'évêque Burnell qui y ajouta le Grand Hall et la chapelle entre 1275 et 1292.

A la suite d'un litige avec la municipalité, l'évêque Ralph construisit au 14e siècle le pont-levis, la loge et la douve. Celle-ci abrite une variété intéressante d'oiseaux, notamment des cygnes qui ont appris à sonner une cloche lorsqu'ils ont faim (photo à droite).

Le palais (photo ci-dessus) est ouvert aux visiteurs du printemps à l'automne, ainsi que certains jours pour des oeuvres de bienfaisance.

Les jardins du palais recouvrant près de 5,5 hectares se composent d'un parterre magnifique de pelouses, parsemées de fleurs, buissons et arbres (photo à droit). En été, sur la pelouse centrale, où se dresse un noyer noir presque bicentenaire, se déroulent les matchs du club de croquet du palais (photo à droite).

DAS BISCHÖFLICHE PALAIS:

DAS BISCHÖFLICHE PALAIS: Bischof Jocelyn, der in Wells zur Welt kam, ist die Gründung des Palais im 13ten Jahrhundert zu verdanken, als er einen Park anlegte und darin eine Gewölbekammer für Wohnunterkünfte baute.

Verschiedene Anbauten wurden von nachfolgenden Bischöfen ausgeführt, speziell von Bischof Burnell, der die Grosse Halle und die Kapelle in den Jahren 1275 bis 1292 hinzufügte.

Nach einer Auseinandersetzung mit den örtlichen Behörden baute Bischof Ralph im 14ten Jahrhundert die Zugbrücke, das Torhaus und den Wassergraben. Der Graben wird von einer interessanten Vielfalt an Wasservögeln bewohnt, einschließlich Schwänen, die gelernt haben, eine Glocke zu läuten, wenn sie Futter haben wollen (Foto Seite 11).

Das Palais (Foto links) ist für Besucher vom Frühling bis zum Herbst einschließlich verschiedener Feiertage, geöffnet.

Die zum Palais gehörigen Gärten erstrecken sich über 14 Morgen und weisen eine herrliche Zusammenstellung von Rasenflächen, Blumen, Sträuchern und Bäumen auf (Foto oben). Auf der zentralen Rasenfläche, auf der ein beinahe zweihundert Jahre alter schwarzer Walnußbaum steht, spielt während der Sommermonate der Palais-Krocketclub (Foto links).

Sufficient remains of the Great Hall (photograph page 13), to show what a grand building it once was. It was 35 metres long and 18 metres wide and the roof was probably supported by two rows of pillars. The Great Hall proved too expensive for Bishops to maintain. In the late 16th century, lead and timber from the roof was sold in order to raise money; thereafter the building was allowed to become a romantic ruin.

Wells derives its name from the wells within the Palace grounds. Bishop Thomas Bekynton (1443-1466) built the well house (also known as the 'conduit' house) as part of the system to supply water to the Palace, and also to the inhabitants of Wells. The public water supply fed a fountain in the Market Place (replaced by the present fountain in the 18th century) and then ran in conduits along the streets as it does to this day.

In return for granting this water supply to the city, Bishop Bekynton requested that a service of thanksgiving should be held annually, when prayers should be said for him. This service, attended by the Mayor and Corporation, is still held in January each year.

Visitors cannot fail to be impressed when entering the ground floor by the magnificent Entrance Hall (photograph below) and Undercroft which run parallel. The vaulted roof and the medieval architecture of this part of the building is well preserved. The Undercroft runs off the Entrance Hall and is now the refectory, though over the years has been put to a number of uses, such as a wine store, a museum, a dining room, and even a coal cellar. The Long Gallery

(photograph page 16) on the first floor suffered considerable damage from Parliamentary troops in the Civil War. It and the original Hall on this upper floor were extensively remodelled in Victorian times to create the present Drawing Room, and Conference Room.

The "Purbeck Marble" columns in the Long Gallery are in fact enamelled iron, while ornate wood carvings on doors and panelling, is really Victorian papier-mache moulding. The Drawing Room was originally open to the rafters but in the mid-19th century a plaster ceiling was installed. A sample is displayed of the green-flock wallpaper used in 1845 and only rediscovered in 1977 when two medieval window embrasures were found behind some bookcases.

The Chapel is the private chapel of the Bishops of Bath and Wells and has for centuries been in constant use daily for worship and prayers. The east window (photograph page 16) was restored by Bishop Law (1824-1845) with a 'cartload' of glass fragments from church windows in and around Rouen in France that had been destroyed or damaged during the French Revolution.

Panelled Room.

Le Grand Hall, autrefois superbe, est aujourd'hui en ruines (photo page 13), mais ses vestiges donnent une impression de son importance de jadis.

Wells tient son nom des puits (wells, en anglais) dispersés dans les jardins du palais. L'évêque Bekynton (1443-1466) construisit la maison du puits dans le cadre d'un système d'alimentation en eau pour le palais, et aussi pour les habitants de la ville de Wells. Ce débit d'eau était dirigé vers une fontaine dressée sur la place du marché, puis le long des rues. On peut encore aujourd'hui voir l'eau du puits s'écouler le long de la grand-rue.

En pénétrant au rez-de-chaussée, les visiteurs ne manqueront pas d'admirer le magnifique Hall d'entrée (photo page 15), et la crypte qui le suit en parallèle. Ils sont surmontés d'une voûte et l'architecture médiévale a été magnifiquement conservée.

Les troupes du Parlement causèrent beaucoup de dégâts dans la Longue Galerie qui occupait autrefois toute la longueur du bâtiment. Après plusieurs années d'abandon, elle fut raccourcie et rénovée à l'époque victorienne.

La division du hall original aboutit à la création du Drawing Room et de la Conference Room. La charpente à chevrons du Drawing Room était apparente autrefois, mais vers le milieu du 19e siècle, elle fut dissimulée par un plafond en plâtre.

La chapelle de l'évêque (photo page 16) est la chapelle privée des évêques de Bath et Wells. Elle fut, pendant des siècles, utilisée quotidiennement pour les services religieux et les prières. Les vitraux du côté Est (photo ci-dessus) constituent une particularité remarquable de la chapelle, car, ayant été dissimulés, il furent restaurés par l'évêque Law (1824-1845) qui, après un voyage à Rouen, ramena une "pleine charrette" de vitraux provenant d'églises qui avaient été détruites ou endommagées pendant la révolution française. Ils ont été mis en place pour former un motif de mosaïque irrégulier.

Die einst phantastische Große Halle ist heute eine Ruine (Foto Seite 13); die überreste lassen jedoch noch erkennen, was für ein großartiges Gebäude es einmal war.

Wells hat seinen Namen von den drei Quellen auf dem Palaisgrundstück. Bischof Bekynton (1443-1466) baute das Brunnenhaus als Teil des Wasserversorgungssystems für das Palais und auch, um die Stadt Wells mit Wasser zu versorgen. Die Wasserleitung ging zu einem Brunnen auf dem Marktplatz und weiter die Straße entlang. Dieses Quellwasser läuft auch heute noch die High Street entlang.

Wenn Besucher das Erdgeschoss betreten, sind sie ausnahmslos von der gewölbten, herrlichen Eingangshalle und der Krypta, die parallel zueinander verlaufen, beeindruckt (Foto Seite 15). Ihre mittelalterliche Architektur ist wunderbar erhalten.

Regierungstruppen fügten der "Long Gallery", (Foto unten) die sich einmal über die gesamte Länge des Gebäudes erstreckte, großen Schaden zu. Nach vielen Jahren der Vernachlässigung wurde sie verkürzt und während der viktorianischen Zeit renoviert.

Durch Unterteilung der ursprünglichen Halle entstanden der Salon und Konferenzraum. Der Salon war ursprünglich bis zu den Dachsparren geöffnet. In der Mitte des 19ten Jahrhunderts wurde eine Gipsdecke eingezogen.

Die Bischofskapelle ist die private Kapelle der Bischöfe von Bath und Wells und ist seit Jahrhunderten ständig für die täglichen Gottesdienste und Gebete benutzt worden. Das Ostfenster ist eine bemerkenswerte Besonderheit der Kapelle (Foto oben). Es war verdeckt worden und wurde von Bischof Law (1824-1845) wiederhergestellt, der nach Rouen reiste und eine Wagenladung Glas von Kirchenfenstern zurückbrachte, die während der französischen Revolution zerstört oder beschädigt worden waren. Er fügte das Glas zu einem willkürlichen Mosaikmuster zusammen.

CATHEDRAL GREEN

Cathedral Green (photograph below), outside the West Front of the Cathedral, was originally allocated as the lay cemetery by statute in 1243. Canons were buried in the Palm churchyard (Cloister Garth), while Vicars Choral (the men of the Choir) were interred in the Camery, east of the Cloisters.

The Green provides a wonderful setting for the ancient houses (photograph page 18), including the Old Deanery, the former Archdeacon's house (now the Wells Cathedral Music School), the Wells Museum, and the Chain Gate, built in 1459.

Wells Museum was formerly a canonical house, traditionally the Chancellor's residence. Behind the present 18th century building, remains of the medieval canon's house have been discovered. Since 1930 it has been the City's museum which contains an excellent local history reference library. Amongst its exhibits is the stuffed body of the first swan to ring the moat bell at the Bishop's gatehouse for its food.

L'ENCLOS DE LA CATHÉDRALE (photo page 17), tourné ver la façade Ouest, était originalement réservé par le décret de 1243 à un cimetière laïque. Les chanoines devaient être enterrés dans la cour de l'église (le cloître de Garth) tandis que les membres du choeur des vicaires étaient enterrés dans la Camery (à l'Est des cloîtres).

L'enclos constitue un décor harmonieux pour les anciennes maisons (photo ci-dessus), et notamment l'ancienne demeure du doyen, l'ancienne résidence de l'archidiacre (maintenant l'école de musique de la cathédrale), le musée de Wells et le pont du Chain Gate, construit en 1459.

Le musée de Wells fut établi au 16e siècle pour servir de résidence au chancelier, mais après la résidence de deux chanceliers seulement, il passa aux mains d'un particulier. Depuis 1930, il abrite un musée qui contient une excellente bibliothèque de référence de l'histoire locale.

DAS CATHEDRAL GREEN (Die Grünfläche neben der Kathedrale): Die Grünfläche (Foto Seite 17) an der westlichen Vorderseite der Kathedrale war ursprünglich durch ein Gesetz von 1243 zum Laienfriedhof bestimmt; Kanoniker sollten im Palmen-Kirchhof (Cloister Garth) bestattet werden, während der Priesterchor in der Camery (Gewölbekammer) östlich der Kreuzgänge beerdigt wurde.

Simes Map 1735,
Wells Museum.

Die Grünfläche bietet einen wunderbaren Rahmen für die historischen Gebäude (Foto oben), einschließlich der alten Dekanei, der Erzdekanei (heute die Musikschule der Kathedrale), des Wells-Museums und des Kettentors, das 1459 gebaut wurde.

Das Wells-Museum wurde im 16ten Jahrhundert als Kanzlerresidenz erbaut, doch nur zwei Kanzler lebten dort, danach ging es in Laienhände über. Seit 1930 ist es ein Museum mit einer ausgezeichneten Referenzbibliothek der örtlichen Geschichte.

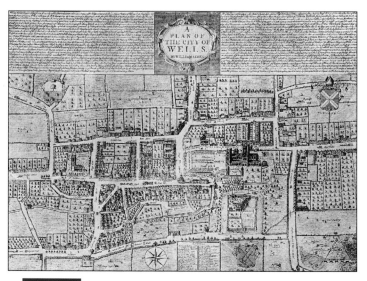

CHAIN GATE

Thomas Bekynton, who was Bishop of Bath and Wells 1443-65, built the Chain Gate and Bridge (photograph below) over the main Bath road, linking the Vicars Hall, and the Chapter House stairs, so that the Vicars Choral avoided having to cross a busy street. It was probably so named because the gateway was occasionally closed with chains.

The external clock, faces the Canons' houses on Cathedral Green.

L'horlage exérieure fait aux maisons des chanoines qui donnent sur l'enclos de la cathédrale.

Die Uhr an der Außeseite zeigt in die Richtung der Kanonikerhäuser die auf den Grünflächen der Kathedrale stehen.

CHAIN GATE: Thomas Bekynton qui était évêque de Bath et de Wells de 1443 à 1463, construisit le pont à chaîne (photo ci-dessous), sur la route principale de Bath. Il relie le Hall du vicaire et l'escalier de la maison du chapitre afin d'éviter au choeur des vicaires d'avoir à traverser une rue très fréquentée.

DAS KETTENTOR: Thomas Bekynton, der von 1443-63 Bischof von Bath und Wells war, baute die Kettenbrücke (Foto unten) über die Hauptstraße von Bath, die die Priesterhalle und die Stufen des Kapitelsaals miteinander verbinden, damit der Priesterchor das überqueren dieser geschäftigen Straße vermeiden konnte.

VICARS' CLOSE

The Vicars' Choral - the gentlemen members of the Cathedral Choir - have been in existence since the 12th century. In 1348 that they were formed into a College community by Bishop Ralph who built the Close, with its Hall and 42 small dwellings to house them (photograph below & right). After the English Reformation in the 16th century, the Vicars' Choral were allowed to marry, so the houses were amalgamated into larger dwellings in order to accommodate their families.

Today other members of the Cathedral staff are also housed in the Close, and four of the houses are used by the Cathedral school.

Two of the houses in St Andrews Street are particularly noteworthy: Tower House is a medieval canonical house which was occupied by the Precentor of the Cathedral, but is now in private occupancy. At the south end of the house there are some 14th century blocked windows. The 16th century tower was probably designed to contain the staircase, with small rooms on the two top floors.

On the other side of St Andrew's Street is The Rib, a handsome 15th century canonical house. It is the only survivor of a number of houses which were in the gift of the Bishop, and these were known locally as "the bishop's ribs". (This is also now privately occupied).

VICAR'S CLOSE: Le choeur des vicaires, les membres privilégiés du choeur de la cathédrale, existe depuis le 12e siècle, mais c'est en 1348 qu'ils furent constitués en une communauté par l'évêque Ralph qui construisit la ruelle de maisons pour les loger (photo pages 20-21). Après les bouleversements religieux du 16e siècle, les membres du Vicars' Choral eurent le droit de se marier. Les maisonnettes furent donc agrandies pour pouvoir accueillir leurs familles.

Deux des maisons de la rue St Andrews sont particulièrement remarquables: La Tower House qui fut occupée de 1337 jusqu'au milieu du 19e siècle par le Grand chantre, mais qui appartient maintenant à des particuliers.

De l'autre côté de la rue St Andrews, une maison, The Rib, fut construite au 15e siècle. Elle fait partie d'une rangée de maisonnettes attribuées au gré de l'évêque, et connues localement sous le nom de "Bishop's Ribs".

DER PRIESTERHOF: Den Priesterchor - den Männerchor der Kathedrale - gibt es seit dem 12ten Jahrhundert, erst 1348 wurde er jedoch von Bischof Ralph zu einer Gemeinschaft zusammengeschlossen. Dieser erbaute auch den Hof, um sie unterzubringen (Foto Seites 20-21). Nach einem religiösen Aufruhr im 16ten Jahrhundert war es den Mitgliedern des Priesterchors erlaubt zu heiraten, daher wurden die Häuser in größere Wohnhäuser umgebaut, um auch ihre Familien unterzubringen.

Zwei Häuser in der St. Andrews Street sind besonders bemerkenswert: Das Tower House wurde von 1337 bis Mitte des 19ten Jahrhunderts vom Vorsänger bewohnt, ist heute aber in Privatbesitz.

Auf der anderen Seite der St. Andrews Street steht ein Haus, das The Rib genannt wird, und im 15ten Jahrhundert erbaut wurde. Es war eines von vielen Häusern, die der Bischof verschenkt hat, und die als "die Bischofsrippe" bekannt waren.

THE MARKET PLACE

The Market Place (photograph below & far right), site of markets and fairs since the 1100s, is the centre of three facets of influence in Wells. The Penniless Porch (photograph right) – so-called because beggars would seek alms from churchgoers – leads into the Liberty, the domain of the Dean and Chapter; the magnificent gate, known as Bishop's Eye, leads to the Palace, and the handsome 18th-century Town Hall is the focus of the City's civic life. In front of some shops near Penniless Porch, marked out in bronze, is the length of the long jump made in the 1964 Olympics by Mary Rand, then a resident of Wells. She won her Gold Medal with a jump of 22 feet 2 ¼ inches (6.77m).

The 15th-century Swan Hotel, in Sadler Street just outside the Market Place, was once an important coaching inn. Its many famous visitors include the wife of James VI and I Queen Anne, who left behind an ornate and rather uncomfortable wooden armchair that is still used to this day for each new mayor's installation ceremony.

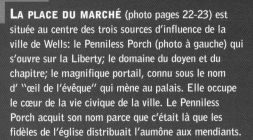

LA PLACE DU MARCHÉ (photo pages 22-23) est située au centre des trois sources d'influence de la ville de Wells: le Penniless Porch (photo à gauche) qui s'ouvre sur la Liberty; le domaine du doyen et du chapitre; le magnifique portail, connu sous le nom d' "œil de l'évêque" qui mène au palais. Elle occupe le cœur de la vie civique de la ville. Le Penniless Porch acquit son nom parce que c'était là que les fidèles de l'église distribuait l'aumône aux mendiants.

Dans Sadler Street, juste devant la place du marché, le Swan Hotel (Hôtel du Cygne) date du 15e siècle et fut jadis un important relais de poste.

DER MARKTPLATZ (Foto Seites 22-23) steht im Mittelpunkt dreier bedeutender Aspekte in Wells: das "Penniless" Portal (Foto links), das in die Liberty, den Sitz des Dekans und Kapitels führt; das prächtige Tor, das als "Bischofsauge" bekannt ist und zum Palais führt; dies ist das Herz des bürgerlichen Lebens der Stadt. Das "Penniless" Portal heißt so, weil hier die Bettler von Kirchengängern Almosen erbettelten.

Das Swan Hotel (Foto links unten), aus dem 15. Jh., in der Sadler Street, in unmittelbarer Nähe vom Marktplatz, war ehemals ein bekannter Gasthof, wo die Postkutschen anhielten.

St. Cuthbert's Church

St. Cuthbert's, the city church of Wells, the largest parish church in Somerset (photograph below), has no certain origins, but it is probable that a church has stood on this site since the 9th century. St Cuthbert himself was a Saxon saint in the days of King Alfred - he who burnt the cakes.

The magnificent church we see today was begun in the 13th century, but is now largely 15th century in appearance, with a particularly fine nave ceiling repainted in medieval colours (photograph right). The western tower, rising to a height of 47 metres, was started in 1410.

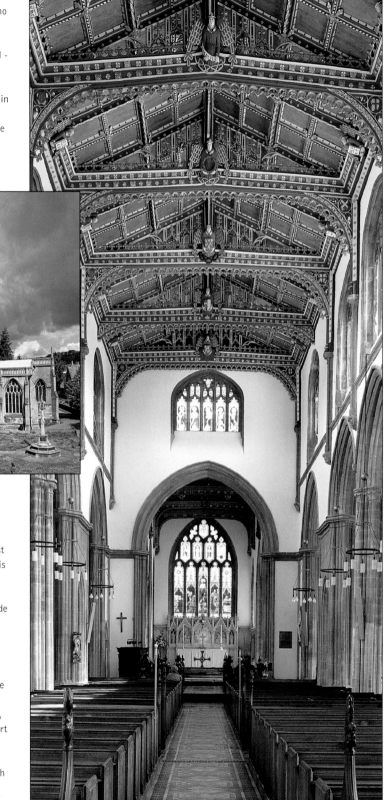

L'ÉGLISE DE ST CUTHBERT: L'origine de St Cuthbert, la plus grande église paroissiale du Somerset (photo ci-dessus), est incertaine, mais il est probable qu'une église se dressait à cet endroit depuis le 9e siècle.

La magnifique église que nous admirons aujourd'hui fut commencé au 13e siècle, mais subit de nombreuses modifications, restaurations et agrandissements au fil des années.

DIE ST. CUTHBERT'S KIRCHE: St. Cuthbert, die größte Gemeindekirche in Somerset (Foto oben), ist unbestimmten Ursprungs, aber es ist wahrscheinlich, dass an dieser Stelle schon seit dem 9ten Jahrhundert eine Kirche gestanden hat.

Der Bau der prächtigen Kirche, die wir heute sehen, wurde im 13ten Jahrhundert begonnen, jedoch sind viele Änderungen, Restaurierungen und Vergrößerungen im Laufe der Jahre daran vorgenommen worden.

BISHOP'S BARN

Originally built as a store for the produce from the Bishop's numerous estates, the Barn is a large heavily buttressed building standing in the Recreation Ground. It was used as a billet for the soldiers guarding the notorious Judge Jeffreys when he was presiding over the "Bloody Assizes" held in the Market Place after Monmouth's Rebellion (the "Pitchfork Rebellion") in 1685.

CITY ARMS

Now a popular public house and restaurant in the High Street, near St. Cuthbert's, The City Arms was, from Tudor times to the 19th century, the City Jail (photograph right).

LA GRANGE ÉPISCOPALE: Originalement construite comme dépôt pour les produits des nombreux domaines de l'évêque, la Barn est un bâtiment à larges contreforts dressé sur la cour de récréation.

LE CITY ARMS: Maintenant un pub et restaurant très fréquenté dans la grand-rue, le City Arms servit, depuis l'époque des Tudor jusqu'au 19e siècle, de prison pour la ville (photo à droite).

DIE BISCHOFS-SCHEUNE: Die Scheune, die ursprünglich als Lagerraum für Landwirtschaftsprodukte von den zahlreichen Höfen des Bischofs erbaut wurde, ist ein großes Gebäude mit schweren Strebepfeilern, das im Freizeitpark steht.

DAS CITY ARMS war von der Tudorzeit bis zum 19ten Jahrhundert das Stadtgefängnis (Foto oben) und ist heute eine beliebte Gaststätte und Restaurant in der High Street.

BUBWITH'S ALMSHOUSES

In the early 15th century Bishop Bubwith endowed these almshouses (photograph below) with the aim of accommodating poor men and women burgesses of the city. Originally a single storey building with a chapel to the east and a hall to the west, there were 12 cubicles, but a first floor was added later thus doubling the accommodation.

BISHOP BUBWITH'S ALMSHOUSES: Au début du 15e siècle, l'évêque Bubwith dota la cathédrale de ces maisons d'indigents (photo ci-dessous) qui devaient héberger les bourgeois appauvris de la ville.

DIE BUBWITH'S ARMENHÄUSER: Im frühen 15ten Jahrhundert stiftete Bishof Bubwith diese Armenhäuser (Foto links), um mittellose Männer und Frauen, die Bürger der Stadt waren, zu beherbergen.

WOOKEY HOLE

Only a mile from Wells are the Wookey Hole Caves which were formed thousands of years ago by the River Axe which eroded the limestone into passages, pools and chambers deep underground. The caves (photograph above) were once occupied by man, and, according to legend, by the Witch of Wookey.

During a guided cave tour, modern electronic wizardry is used to bring to life for the first time the legendary Witch of Wookey Hole when visitors come face to face with the witch as the star of a spectacular magic and light show.

After touring the caves visitors can watch a film on the history of papermaking and try their hand at making a sheet of handmade paper in a Victorian papermill (photograph above) and then visit a Magical Mirror Maze, Edwardian Penny Arcade, museum and working waterwheel.

WOOKEY HOLE: A 1,5 km seulement de Wells, les grottes de Wookey Hole furent creusées il y plusieurs siècles par la rivière Axe qui éroda le calcaire pour former des tunnels, des étangs et des chambres souterraines profondes. Les grottes (photo ci-dessus) furent jadis occupées par l'homme et, selon la légende, par la sorcière de Wookey.

Après une visite guidée des grottes, les visiteurs peuvent regarder un film retraçant l'histoire de la fabrication du papier (photo à gauche), puis visiter un labyrinthe de miroirs magiques, la Penny Arcade édouardienne, un musée et un moulin à papier en état de marche.

WOOKEY HOLE: Nur eine Meile von Wells entfernt befinden sich die Wookey Hole Höhlen. Vor Jahrhunderten bildete der Fluß Axe Durchgänge, unterirdische Seen und Kammern, indem er tief im Untergrund den Kalkstein auswusch. Die Höhlen (Foto oben) wurden einst von Menschen bewohnt und, wie die Legende sagt, von der Hexe von Wookey.

Nach einer Höhlenführung können Besucher einen Film über die Geschichte der Papierherstellung sehen (Foto links) und ein magisches Spiegellabyrinth, die Edwardian Penny Arcade, das Museum und ein in Betrieb befindliches Wasserrad besuchen.

MILTON LODGE GARDENS

Half a mile north of Wells, on the Old Bristol Road, these gardens (photograph below) are open to the public daily from Easter to the end of October. First began in 1909, as a mature alkaline terraced garden, it was re-planned in 1962 with a beautiful variety of flowers, shrubs, trees and yew hedges. There is a 7 acre arboretum on the opposite side of the Old Bristol Road.

Les jardins de Milton Lodge: A 800 m, au nord de Wells, sur l'ancienne route de Bristol, ces jardins (photo ci-dessous) sont ouverts tous les jours au public, de Pâques à la fin du mois d'octobre. Ils contiennent une magnifique variété de fleurs, buissons, arbres et bordures d'if.

Die Milton Lodge Gärten: Diese Gärten liegen eine halbe Meile nördlich von Wells an der Old Bristol Road. Sie (Foto unten) sind für die Öffentlichkeit von Ostern bis Ende Oktober geöffnet und bieten eine wunderbare Vielfalt an Blumen, Büschen, Bäumen und Eibenhecken.

AROUND WELLS

CHEDDAR

Eight miles west of Wells is the Cheddar Gorge (photograph right & page 28) which runs for almost a mile from Cheddar Village up into the Mendip Hills. The cliffs rise to over 137 metres. Cox's Cave, discovered in 1837, and Gough's Cave, discovered in 1877, are called after the local men who first found them.

Cheddar gives its name to the world famous cheese, made in the area since medieval times.

Glastonbury

Glastonbury is traditionally regarded as the cradle of Christianity in England. The first church was built of wattles in about 600AD, round which St Dunstan built a new Abbey during the years 940-957. In 1184 a fire consumed much of the Abbey, but it was lavishly rebuilt. Although destroyed in the Dissolution of the Monasteries in 1539,the remains are still worth a visit (photograph below).

One part of the domestic quarters survive almost intact, a great rarity: the Abbot's Kitchen, dating from the 14th century. Here meals were prepared for the Abbot and his guests.

Legend has it that Joseph of Arimathea buried the Holy Grail somewhere in the area now called Chalice Well. The Glastonbury Thorn is a hawthorn tree which is said to have originated when Joseph drove his walking staff into the ground on Wirral Hill, where it miraculously took root, and still flowers at Christmas.

Dans les environs de Wells

CHEDDAR: A 12 km de Wells, la Cheddar Gorge (photo page 27 et ci-dessus) s'étale sur près d'1,5 km du village de Cheddar dans les Mendip Hills. Les falaises s'élèvent à plus de 135 mètres.

Cheddar donne son nom aux fromages qui, à une certaine époque, étaient entreposés dans ces grottes aux conditions idéales.

Die Umgebung von Wells

CHEDDAR: 8 Meilen von Wells liegt Cheddar Gorge, die Schlucht von Cheddar (Foto Seite 27 und oben), die sich fast eine Meile vom Dorf Cheddar bis in die Mendip Hügel hinzieht. Die Felsen sind über 150m hoch.

Cheddar gibt dem Käse seinen Namen, der früher auf Grund der idealen Bedingungen in den Höhlen gelagert wurde.

GLASTONBURY: Glastonbury Abbey, traditionnellement le sanctuaire chrétien le plus ancien des îles britanniques, est considéré comme le berceau de la chrétienté en Angleterre. Autour de la première église construite en clayonnages vers l'an 600, St Dunstan construisit une nouvelle abbaye pendant les années 940-857. En 1184, un incendie ravagea la plus grande partie des bâtiments et la reconstruction ultérieure de l'abbaye dura plus de 300 ans. Bien que détruite lors de la dissolution des ordres monastiques en 1539, les vestiges valent bien la visite (photo à gauche).

GLASTONBURY: Die Abtei von Glastonbury ist das älteste, traditionelle christliche Heiligtum auf den britischen Inseln und wird als Wiege des christlichen Glaubens in England angesehen. Die erste Kirche wurde ungefähr im Jahre 600 AD aus Flechtwerk erbaut, während der Jahre 940-957 baute St. Dunstan eine neue Abtei. 1184 brannte das Gebäude nahezu ab, und der darauffolgende Wiederaufbau blieb über 300 Jahre erhalten. Obwohl die Abtei bei der Auflösung des Mönchsklosters im Jahre 1539 zerstört wurde, sind die überreste noch immer einen Besuch wert (Foto links).

GLASTONBURY TOR

The distinctive Tor (photograph right) is visible from all directions, and on a misty morning looks as if it were an island in a lake. On the summit is the remains of St Michael's Chapel, of which only the tower is intact. Visitors who make the strenuous climb to the top of the Tor are rewarded, on a clear day, with one of the finest views in Britain.

GLASTONBURY TOR: Le Tor (photo à droite) est visible de toutes les directions. Par un matin brumeux, il ressemble à une île au milieu d'un lac. Bien que ce soit une grimpée assez éprouvante, les visiteurs qui parviennent au sommet du Tor sont récompensés par l'un des plus beaux panoramas de Grande-Bretagne.

Glastonbury Tor: Glastonbury Tor (Foto rechts) ist ein Berg, der von allen Richtungen aus zu sehen ist. An einem nebligen Morgen wirkt er wie eine Insel in einem See. Obwohl es ein ziemlicher Konditionstest ist, werden Besucher, die es bis an die Spitze des Berges schaffen, mit einer der malerischsten Aussichten von England belohnt.

LONGLEAT

Longleat, regarded as one of England's finest country houses (photograph below), has been the home of the Thynne family, Marquises of Bath, for over 400 years. Set in a glorious parkland with a lakeside setting, it was built in the Renaissance style and completed in 1580 by Sir John Thynne who acted as his own architect.

In 1947 it was one of the first stately homes to be opened to the public, and the Safari Park was the first of its kind in Britain.

LONGLEAT

, qui est considéré comme l'un des plus beaux manoirs de l'Angleterre (photo ci-dessous) abrite la famille Thynne depuis plus de 400 ans. Erigé dans un superbe parc paysagé avec un lac, dans le style de la renaissance, il fut achevé en 1580 par Sir John Thynne qui en fut l'architecte principal.

LONGLEAT

wird als eines der schönsten Landhäuser Englands angesehen (Foto unten), und war über 400 Jahre lang Sitz der Familie Thynne. Es liegt in einer herrlichen Parkanlage an einem See. Sir John Thynne, der selbst als Architekt wirkte, erbaute es im Renaissancestil. Es wurde im Jahre 1580 fertiggestellt.

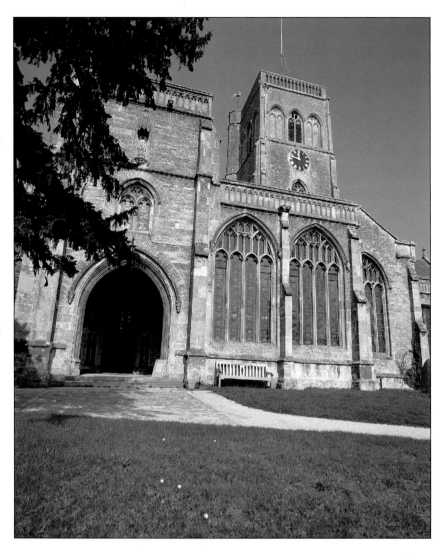

WEDMORE

It was here that peace was agreed between King Alfred and the Danes in 878 AD.
A beautiful village to wander around, there are a number of period properties. The Perpendicular Church of St. Mary Magdalene (photograph above) contains many fascinating features.

WEDMORE: Joli village pour une promenade, avec plusieurs propriétés anciennes. L'église de style perpendiculaire de St Mary Magdalene (photo ci-dessus) contient plusieurs objets fascinants.

WEDMORE: Eine wunderschönes Dorf zum Spazierengehen, mit einer Reihe von zeitgenössischen Gebäuden. Die perpendikulare Kirche von St. Mary Magdalene (Foto oben) bietet viele faszinierende Besonderheiten.

CHEWTON MENDIP

The Chewton Cheese Dairy at Chewton Mendip, 5 miles from Wells, is one of the last farmhouse cheese dairies making traditional Cheddar cheese (photograph right). It is open to visitors to watch this process and they can also enjoy the Woodland Garden and Parkland for walks and picnics.

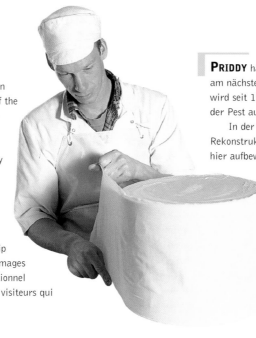

CHEWTON CHEESE: La Chewton Cheese Dairy située à Chewton Mendip est l'une des dernières laiteries de fromages fermiers fabriquant du cheddar traditionnel (photo à droite). Elle est ouverte aux visiteurs qui peuvent assister à la fabrication.

CHEWTON KÄSE: Die Chewton Käserei in Chewton Mendip ist eine der letzten Farmhaus Käsereien die den traditionellen Cheddar Käse produzieren (Foto oben). Sie ist für Besucher geöffnet, die den Herstellungsprozess verfolgen können.

PRIDDY

Priddy holds an annual sheep fair on the Wednesday nearest to 21st August. It has done so ever since 1348 when the fair was moved out from Wells because of the plague, the "Black Death".

In the middle of the village green is a thatched stack of the hurdles (photograph right) used to form the sheep pens at the time of the fair. Local legend has it that the fair will only survive if these hurdles are preserved.

To the north-east of the village are the Priddy Nine Barrows. These were pre-historic burial mounds. A little further away are three huge pre-historic earthen circles, each some 183 metres in diameter. Their exact purpose is still a mystery.

PRIDDY organise une foire des moutons annuelle, le mercredi le plus proche du 21 août. Cette tradition remonte à 1348 date à laquelle la foire de Wells y fut transférée à cause de la Peste Noire.

Au milieu de la place pelousée du village, on peut voir une reconstruction des claies (photo ci-dessus) qui y étaient entreposées pour servir de clôtures au moment de la foire des moutons.

PRIDDY hält an dem Mittwoch, der dem 21. August am nächsten liegt, jährlich eine Schafsmesse ab. Dies wird seit 1348 praktiziert, nachdem die Messe wegen der Pest aus Wells heraus verlegt wurde.

In der Mitte der Dorfwiese ist eine Rekonstruktion der Hürden zu sehen (Foto unten), die hier aufbewahrt wurden, um die Schafpferche für die Schafmesse aufzubauen.

FLEET AIR ARM MUSEUM, YEOVILTON

The Fleet Air Arm Museum (photograph below) is one of the world's leading museums, illustrating the history of British Naval Aviation from 1908 to the present day. It has over 80 aircraft in its collection, 40 of which are on permanent display. A major exhibition is the award-winning "Carrier" - a flight-deck on land with eleven carrier-borne aircraft.

MUSÉE DE L'ARMÉE DE L'AIR, YEOVILTON: Le Musée de l'armée de l'air (photo ci-dessous) est l'un des plus importants musées du monde, illustrant l'histoire de l'aéronavale britannique depuis 1908 jusqu'à nos jours. Sa collection renferme plus de 80 avions dont 40 sont en présentation permanente. Une exposition remarquable est celle du "Carrier" primé (une escadrille sur terre comptant onze avions sur porte-avions).

LUFTWAFFEN-MUSEM, YEOVILTON: Das Luftwaffen-Museum (Foto unten) ist eins der führenden Museen der Welt, das die Geschichte der britischen Militärluftfahrt von 1908 bis zum heutigen Tag illustriert. Es hat über 80 Flugzeuge in seiner Sammlung, davon sind 40 permanent ausgestellt. Ein Hauptausstellungsstück ist der preisgekrönte "Carrier" - ein Flugzeugträgerdeck an Land mit elf dazugehörigen Flugzeugen.

SOMERSET LEVELS

Lying west and south of the Mendips, the Somerset Levels are one of the largest wetlands in Britain. They are low-lying meadows criss-crossed with 'rhynes', a local word for ditches, which are flooded during the winter months and attract many species of birdlife, including Berwick's swans from Siberia. During the summer the Levels have a wealth of wild flowers, due in no small measure to the fact that they have been designated as an 'environmentally sensitive area'.

SOMERSET LEVELS: A l'ouest des Mendip Hills, les Somerset Levels constituent l'un des plus vastes marécages de Grande-Bretagne. Ces prairies en contrebas sillonnées de "rhynes", description locale de rigoles complètement inondées en hiver, qui attirent de nombreuses espèces d'oiseaux.

DIE SOMERSET EBENEN: Westlich der Mendip Hügel liegt die Ebene von Somerset. Sie bildet eins der größten Feuchtgebiete Großbritanniens und besteht aus tiefliegenden Wiesen, die von "rhynes", (einem ortsüblichen Wort für Graben), kreuzförmig durchsetzt sind. Während der Wintermonate werden diese überflutet und ziehen dadurch viele Vogelarten an.